$23.93

D0810987

FEARSOME, SCARY, AND CREEPY ANIMALS

Fierce Cats

Elaine Landau

Enslow Publishers, Inc.

40 Industrial Road	PO Box 38
Box 398	Aldershot
Berkeley Heights, NJ 07922	Hants GU12 6BP
USA	UK

http://www.enslow.com

For Norman Pearl

Library of Congress Cataloging-in-Publication Data

Landau, Elaine.
  Fierce cats / Elaine Landau.
    p. cm. — (Fearsome, scary, and creepy animals)
Summary: Introduces lions and tigers and why they sometimes attack
humans, and tells of some real-life attacks by big cats.
  ISBN 0-7660-2062-2 (hardcover : alk. paper)
 1. Tigers—Juvenile literature. 2. Lions—Juvenile literature. 3.
Tiger attacks--Juvenile literature. 4. Lion attacks—Juvenile
literature. [1. Tigers. 2. Lions. 3. Tiger attacks. 4. Lion attacks.]
I. Title. II. Series.
QL737.C23 L357 2003
599.75—dc21

                                2002006936

Printed in the United States of America

10 9 8 7 6 5 4 3 2 1

To Our Readers:
We have done our best to make sure all Internet addresses in this book were active and appropriate when we went to press. However, the author and the publisher have no control over and assume no liability for the material available on those Internet sites or on other Web sites they may link to. Any comments or suggestions can be sent by e-mail to comments@enslow.com or to the address on the back cover.

Illustration Credits:
  © 1999 Artville, LLC, pp. 24, 35; © Bill Edwards/Brand X Pictures, pp. 16, 17, 22–23 (background); © Corel Corporation, pp. 6, 14, 19, 22 (top), 23 (bottom), 28, 32, 34, 36, 41; © Digital Vision Ltd., pp. ii, iii, 7 (inset), 8, 10, 11, 12, 13, 20, 21, 27, 31 (bottom), 39 (right side), 40, 42, 43, 44; © Field Museum, Neg. #Z94352c, Photographer: John Weinstein, p. 25; John Bavaro, pp. 4, 5; John Moore/Associated Press, p. 30; Picture Quest, pp. i, 38–39 (background). Borders and backgrounds © Corel Corporation, unless otherwise noted.

Cover Illustration: Picture Quest

Contents

1 **An Event at the Zoo** 7

2 **Powerful Cats** 16

3 **Attack!** 22

4 **Tiger Terror** 30

5 **Life as a Big Cat** 38

Fast Facts About Fierce Cats 45

Glossary 46

**Further Reading and
Internet Addresses** 47

Index 48

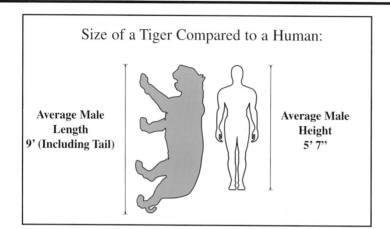

Size of a Tiger Compared to a Human:

Average Male Length 9' (Including Tail)

Average Male Height 5' 7"

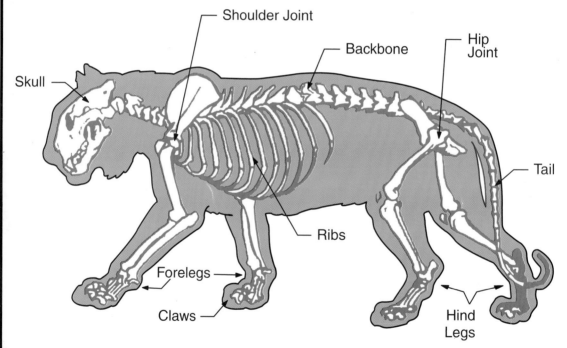

Shoulder Joint

Backbone

Hip Joint

Skull

Tail

Ribs

Forelegs

Claws

Hind Legs

The tiger is the largest member of the cat family. Male tigers grow to be about ten feet long. Female tigers grow to be about eight feet long.

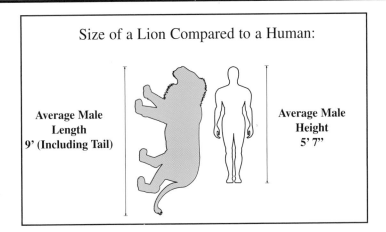

Size of a Lion Compared to a Human:

Average Male Length 9' (Including Tail)

Average Male Height 5' 7"

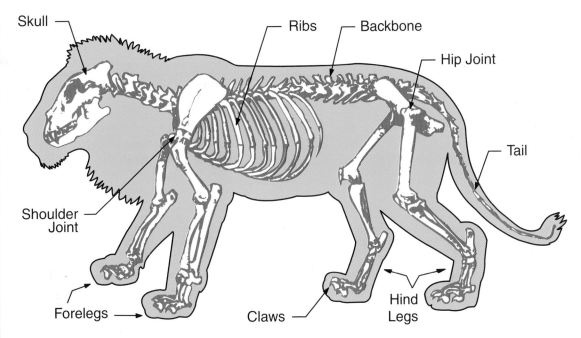

Skull

Ribs

Backbone

Hip Joint

Tail

Shoulder Joint

Forelegs

Claws

Hind Legs

Lions are powerful cats that are strong but not especially fast. Adult males are usually about nine feet long. Adult females are usually about a foot shorter.

1. An Event at the Zoo

It should have been an evening of fun. A large group of people had come to Zoo Boise in Idaho. Everyone was there for a special event. The zoo was having a fundraiser. People came to donate, or give money, to the zoo. They also came to see the animals.

Jan Gold had always loved animals. She had two dogs and two cats at home. She also had a parrot. Gold was at the fundraiser. During the event, she and six friends took a zoo tour.

Jan Gold was taking a tour of Zoo Boise when she found unexpected danger.

The zoo manager led the group. He was going to feed "the boys." These boys were not children. They were two Siberian tigers named Tiaga and Tundra. The tigers were only three years old. But there was nothing small about them. Both of these wildcats were large and powerful. Each weighed about 600 pounds.

The group came to where the tigers were kept. Usually, the animals ate and slept in pens that were always tightly shut. There was a padlock on

Siberian tigers have large, powerful jaws and teeth.

them to stop the tigers from getting out.

But that night, something had gone terribly wrong. Gold was the first to enter the area. She saw that one of pens had been left wide open. Gold reached out to close it. That was a mistake. Suddenly, she was face-to-face with a large tiger. It was Tiaga.

Gold tried not to panic. She did not run. That would have been a bad move. The tiger might think of her as his prey, or food. Instead, Gold backed up slowly.

She tried to calmly leave the pen. But Gold turned her back on the tiger as she left. That was when it happened. Tiaga reached out and grabbed her shoulder.

The tiger knocked the woman to her knees. Gold later remembered that the animal's paw was about "the size of a dinner plate."

Seconds later, Tiaga bit the back of Gold's head. At first, Gold did not feel pain. But she could hear the tiger's teeth scraping on her bone.

A police officer had been on the zoo tour with Gold. He had his gun with him. He fired the weapon into the air to scare the tiger.

It worked. Tiaga climbed off Jan Gold. The tiger

Jan Gold did not run when she was face-to-face with the tiger. She backed slowly away so that the tiger would not think of her as prey.

ran back into its pen. But the danger was not over. Now Tundra, the other tiger, came out. Unfortunately, Tiaga followed Tundra's lead. He came back out, as well.

The police officer fired his gun for a third time. The trick worked again. Both tigers returned to their pen. The zookeeper hurriedly locked the gate.

Gold was still on the ground. She knew she was safe now. Yet, she was afraid that one of the tigers had been shot. Jan Gold did not realize what actually happened. She had been hit by the last bullet. It had bounced off the side of the pen and struck her.

An ambulance was called. At the hospital, three

doctors worked on Gold. Her head had been bleeding badly. The bullet broke her leg in two places. Luckily, she recovered.

That was not the only close call at a zoo. There have been some dangerous incidents with lions as well. One happened at the Bronx Zoo in New York City. Many of the exhibits there look like real wildlife settings. However, there are always barriers to protect the public.

But the barriers have not always been enough when someone tries to get past them. That is how it was for a thirty-two-year-old man who visited the zoo with his mother.

Hundreds of lions live in zoos throughout the world.

The mother and son had been looking at the animals. Suddenly, the man left his mother's side. He jumped over a five-foot-high fence. From there, he climbed about twelve feet up to the animal holding area. Then, he bounded over a second fence. That brought him to the top of the building where the lions were kept.

Two African lions were below. They weighed nearly 350 pounds each. At that point, it was still not too late. The man could have left safely. That did not happen, though.

Male lions usually weigh from 350 to 400 pounds, but some weigh up to 500 pounds.

He climbed down to where the huge cats were. At the time, no one knew why, but it was later learned that the man was mentally ill.

Luckily, the lions did not attack immediately. But they did not ignore him, either. They slowly approached the man. Meanwhile, a police officer arrived on the scene, along with a zookeeper. The zookeeper lured one of the lions away from the man.

The other lion swatted the man's head with its paw. The man was about to hit back when

Lions try to avoid contact with humans. They usually only attack if they are provoked, or bothered.

the police officer called out to him. He told the man to lie on the ground and curl into a ball. Fortunately, the man did as he was told.

But the lion was not quite ready to walk away. It pawed the man's head and chewed his trousers. The animal even started to go for his neck.

The zookeeper came to the rescue. He called out to the curious lion. Within minutes, he coaxed it into backing off. Then, he lured the lion back into its pen.

The man who had entered the lion's area was taken to a hospital. His injuries were not serious. He was treated for scratches on his face and scalp. Things could have been much worse for him.

2. Powerful Cats

Lions and tigers are members of the cat family. They are related to house cats. In many ways, however, lions and tigers are nothing like house cats.

One big difference is size. The tiger is the largest member of the cat family. Male tigers are about ten feet long. Three feet of that is the animal's tail. These powerful cats weigh between 400 and 600 pounds.

A female tiger is called a tigress. Female tigers are smaller than males. They are about eight feet long. They usually weigh between 220 and 375 pounds.

Tigers have beautiful coats. Those living in colder areas have longer, thicker coats. Most tigers' coats are brownish-yellow or orange. They have black stripe markings. Tigers are the only big cats with stripes.

Each tiger's stripes form its own pattern. No two tiger's stripes are alike. A tiger's stripes are like a human's fingerprints. Everyone's fingerprints are different, too.

A tiger has white fur on its throat, belly, and the inside of its legs. A small number of tigers have white fur over most of their bodies. These tigers have dark brown or black stripe markings. There are not many of these tigers in the wild. However, they can often be seen in zoos.

Each tiger has a different stripe pattern.

Lions are magnificent cats, too. People around the world admire them. Tigers are the largest cats, but lions are the second largest. Lions are about nine feet long. Most weigh about 350 pounds. The females are a bit smaller than the males. They are about eight feet long. A female lion is called a lioness.

Lions are extremely strong. Their shoulders and front legs are very muscular. Their hind legs are powerful, as well.

Lions have golden tan coats. Male lions have manes. This is a thick ring of hair that covers the animal's head, neck, shoulders, and chest.

A lion's mane is useful. It makes the lion look powerful. That can frighten other animals.

Did you know...

A lion's mane is not fully grown until the animal is five years old.

18

The lion's mane makes him look even bigger and stronger than he is.

The lion's long mane also gives it protection. It shields the lion's body during fights.

Lions and tigers are good hunters. They have keen senses of hearing and smell. This helps them find prey.

Both lions and tigers have large front paws. There are five toes on each paw. Their claws can be pulled in when walking. This helps keep them razor sharp.

Sharp claws help these animals seize and pull down their prey. Lions and tigers also have large, strong teeth. Each of these animals has thirty teeth. Their teeth are about two or three inches long. These big cats also have powerful jaws with which they kill their prey.

A lion or tiger usually watches its victim while hidden from view. The lion's tan color blends in well with dead grass. A tiger's orange-brown coat and black stripes also blends with its forest surroundings. These large cats slowly creep up on their prey. Then, they make their final charge.

Lions and tigers often only make one or two kills a week. After killing their prey, they drag it to a quiet shaded area. There, they eat their fill. They hide the rest of their prey by using their paws to cover the dead animal with dirt and grass. This stops other animals from eating it. The lion or tiger may come back to the prey for several days. It stops by for small meals.

Tigers are bigger than lions, but lions may be stronger. Who would win in a fight? Most experts say that the lion would kill the tiger.

Female lions are smaller than males.

3.
Attack!

Tigers walk slowly and silently while stalking their prey.

The sun has set. A tiger stands silently in the dry, yellowed brush. It is hard to see the tiger, but the tiger is looking at everything around it. It has begun to hunt.

The tiger looks for a weaker animal, such as one that is young or sick. It stalks the area around a waterhole. The tiger may catch an animal stopping for a drink.

Less than twenty minutes later, it happens. The tiger spots a deer. The deer drinks from the waterhole. It never sees the tiger standing motionless nearby.

Then, suddenly, the tiger attacks. It rushes forward from the rear. The tiger grasps the deer's shoulder with its paw. The deer kicks at the tiger. It is fighting for its life. But the large cat does not release its grip.

The tiger pulls its prey to the ground. It seizes the deer's throat with its powerful jaws. The tiger bites down on the deer's windpipe. The deer cannot breathe. A moment later, the prey is dead.

The tiger drags the deer's body to a nearby spot. The grass is thick there. Now the tiger feasts on its kill.

Hungry tigers often prey on deer.

Before the night is over, it has eaten nearly seventy pounds of the kill.

Tigers and lions are fierce predators. They kill and eat other animals to live. But are humans easy targets for these large cats? People have never been a normal part of a lion's or tiger's diet. Yet, at times, humans have become their prey.

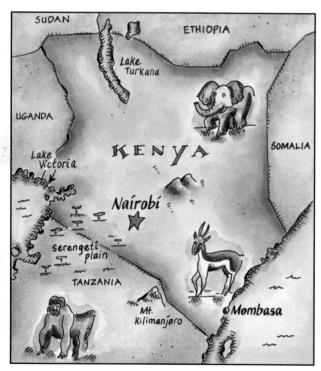

One of the most famous lion attacks took place more than 100 years ago. The trouble began in Kenya in March of 1898. Kenya is a country in Africa. At the

One of the most famous lion attacks in history took place in Kenya, Africa.

24

time, the country of Great Britain owned and controlled the area. The British were building a railway bridge over the Tsavo River. But the work had to stop for a time. The workers were being attacked by lions.

Two lions were involved in these incidents. The native workers named them Ghost and Darkness. At first, only one

The skins of Ghost and Darkness can be seen at the Field Museum of Natural History in Chicago, Illinois.

male lion attacked at night. It would quietly enter the workers' tents. Then, it would drag a screaming victim off into the darkness.

But before long, the lion appeared with another male lion. The pair began attacking together. As the months passed, the lions grew bolder. They began to attack during the day, too. Sometimes, they herded the terrified men into a group. One unlucky worker would become their victim.

Lieutenant Colonel John Henry Patterson was the chief engineer at the site. He, along with the crew, tried to stop the attacks. They fired their guns into the air hoping to scare off the dangerous

Did you know...

○ Both lions and tigers live about twenty years in the wild.

○

○

cats. Campfires were built at night to keep the lions away. Thorn fences and traps were constructed, as well.

The results were disappointing. The lion attacks continued. Patterson had tried to shoot the lions many times. At last, on December 9, 1898, he hit one. Three weeks later, he killed the second. Unfortunately, by then nearly 140 people had been killed.

People still talk about the 1898 incident. It raised many questions. Lions do not usually eat humans. So why did it happen?

No one knows for sure. But scientists have some

The lion has no teeth for chewing. It swallows its food whole.

Lions try to hide their kill from other animals. But sometimes vultures and other animals will wait nearby to eat whatever is left when the lion leaves.

ideas that they developed after studying the lions' skulls. Some scientists think that the lions suffered from painful toothaches. Both animals had some broken teeth. They seem to have had other tooth and gum problems, as well.

Such problems would have made hunting difficult. The lions could not easily crush a large animal's throat. It would be hard for them to attack their usual prey.

Ill or wounded animals usually look for weaker prey, and humans may seem ideal. One scientist told why: "Humans are easy prey. We're very slow, we don't hear very well, and we don't see very well in the dark."

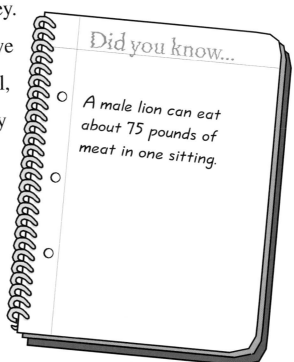

Did you know...

A male lion can eat about 75 pounds of meat in one sitting.

4. Tiger Terror

In some parts of the world, tiger attacks on humans are not uncommon. This is especially true in West Bengal, India. That is where the Sundarbans Tiger Reserve is located.

Tiger hunting is not permitted in this area. As a result, about 500 tigers live in the reserve. It is the world's largest surviving tiger group.

Only scientists and staff members are allowed deep

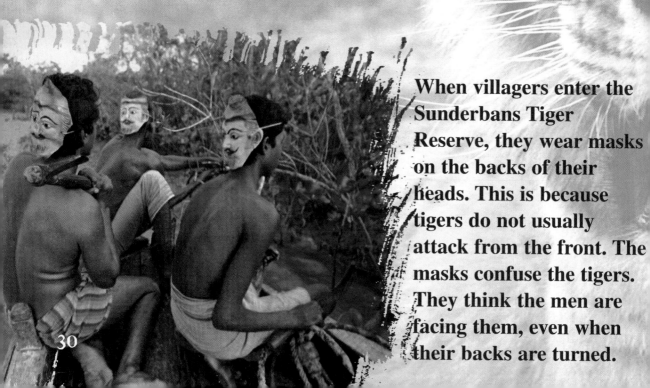

When villagers enter the Sunderbans Tiger Reserve, they wear masks on the backs of their heads. This is because tigers do not usually attack from the front. The masks confuse the tigers. They think the men are facing them, even when their backs are turned.

within the reserve. This protects people from the tigers. It also protects the tigers from being hunted. Individuals are allowed to enter the forest's outer edges. But they need a permit to do so.

The outer edges of the forest are still very dangerous. Tigers have been known to attack people there. Yet, local villagers continue to apply for permits. That is because the area is rich in natural resources.

The waters of the Sundarbans are teeming with fish and prawns. Much of this fish is sold to various areas in Southeast Asia. People also enter the forest to collect the honey that wild bees there produce. Lastly, people come for wood. The forest timber is used for building. It is also used as fuel.

Villagers enter the forest

Tigers have been known to attack people on the outer edges of the forest.

fearfully. Many pray at shrines at the forest's edge beforehand.

Some workers have been attacked by tigers. Often, others watched in horror as it happened. They say they never knew that a tiger was stalking their group. Then, suddenly, it was too late.

This problem is not new. Tigers lived in the Sundarbans even before it was a reserve. At that time, people could work anywhere in the forest. The reported deaths from tiger attacks were extremely high. In the 1930s, tigers attacked as many as 1,500 people a year.

The tigers sometimes even left the forest. They would stalk the surrounding villages. The local people tried to protect themselves. Sometimes they loudly beat drums. They hoped that this would chase the tigers away. But that did not always work. In some cases, people still became victims.

Did you know...

A tiger can drag prey weighing hundreds of pounds nearly a quarter of a mile.

Some tigers were well known for their attacks. These were called man-eaters. One famous man-eater was a female tiger. Her name was Champawat.

Champawat was born in Nepal. Nepal is an Asian country just north of India. That is where Champawat first became known as a man-eater. She killed over 200 people. Quite a few hunters went after Champawat, but they were unable to kill her. Eventually, they were able to chase the tigress out of the country.

Champawat went south to India, where she continued to prey on people. Before long, the tiger more than doubled her number of human victims.

Her last victim was a sixteen-year-old girl. The teenager was out gathering wood when Champawat attacked. The girl's death frightened the villagers. They were afraid to go out.

Tigers usually attack from the rear and go for the neck or throat of their prey.

Champawat became known as a man-eater in Nepal, a country between India and China.

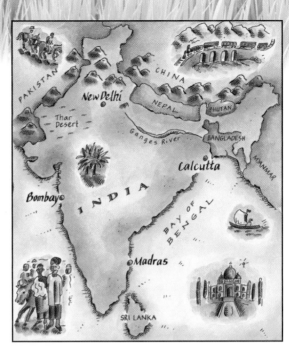

Champawat continued to roam through the area. Sometimes, she would stop on a village road and roar loudly. After many months, Champawat was finally hunted down. The tigress was killed in 1937 by famed tiger hunter Jim Corbett, who only hunted tigers who had become man-killers.

Tiger Attacks

Man-eating tigers sound scary. But they are rare. Just three out of every 1,000 tigers ever attack humans. Such attacks usually occur for specific reasons. Often, this is

true for lion attacks as well. These are a few of the possible causes:

Old Age or Poor Health

Often, older or ill tigers and lions prey on humans. They are too weak to seek out stronger prey. Large cats that prey on humans sometimes have tooth or jaw problems.

Shortage of Usual Prey

Sometimes, there is an outbreak of wildlife disease in the area. Large numbers of animals die. These may include the tiger's and lion's usual prey. With fewer animals around, there is little for the large cats to eat. So, they have to look for other food. They may begin to prey on livestock. These are animals that farmers keep. Village farmers may become victims, too.

Poor Burial Practices

At times, human corpses have not been buried properly. Some bodies were placed in shallow graves. Others were just left out in the open. Tigers and lions have fed on these corpses. It was an easy meal for them. They became used to thinking of people as food.

This happened during the Vietnam War, a war in Southeast Asia during the 1960s and 1970s. Soldiers who were killed in the jungle were not always buried at once. Their bodies were sometimes eaten by tigers. These big cats began to see humans as prey. They attacked living soldiers, as well.

5. Life as a Big Cat

You may have seen lions and tigers in zoos, in movies, and in books. These magnificent animals are found in the wild, as well. But they are not found in as many places as they once were.

Through the years, many of these large cats have died out. They have been hunted for sport and killed for their skins.

Today, lions still live in South and East Central Africa. There are also a few hundred lions left in India. Tigers are still found in most Asian countries.

Tigers usually live in thick forests, but they can be found in many different climates. They live in hot, steamy rain forests or snowy forests. Tigers sometimes also live in swamps, marshes, and tall grasslands. These animals are often found near water.

Tigers live alone. Male tigers mark their territory.

They spray a mixture of urine and scent on trees and bushes. Tigers also scratch trees along the boundaries. Such markings serve as warnings to tell other male tigers to stay away.

However, male tigers will remain close to female tigers. A male tiger's territory often overlaps or is mixed with that of two or three females.

Unlike tigers, lions do not live in thick forests. They prefer broad, open places.

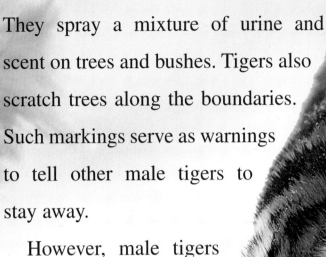

Lions are usually found on grassy plains and open woodlands.

Lions live in groups called prides. A pride is made up of male, female, and young lions. There are ten or more lions in some prides. Like tigers, lions mark off the pride's territory.

The diets of lions and tigers are somewhat alike. But these big cats often hunt differently. Tigers hunt alone. Lions hunt with their prides. Female lions are lighter and swifter. They

Tigers scratch on trees to warn other tigers to stay away.

do most of the hunting. The females share the kill with the pride.

Both lions and tigers usually eat big animals like deer and antelope. Their prey often depends on what animals live in the area. Lions usually eat zebras, buffalo, and warthogs. Tigers eat wild cattle and wild pigs. At times, tigers also eat monkeys and even frogs. Both lions and tigers will eat turtles and fish. Lions and tigers can also be scavengers. They feed on dead animals they find in the wild.

Mating

All large cats mate in much the same way. At the start, the animals roar and paw each other.

Warthogs are wild African pigs with large tusks.

41

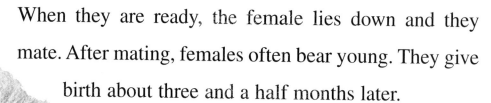

When they are ready, the female lies down and they mate. After mating, females often bear young. They give birth about three and a half months later.

Young lions and tigers are called cubs. Newborn cubs are completely helpless. They are born blind and weigh just a few pounds. At first, the cubs drink their mother's milk. Later, the mother brings them meat. Lion and tiger cubs do not begin to hunt until they are about two years old.

Not every cub lives. Nearly 80 percent of young lions die before they are two years old. Their mothers cannot hunt enough prey to feed all of them. At times, female lions will eat and let their young starve. This is not so for tigers. A mother tiger feeds her cubs first.

Will there always be lions and tigers? Some African nations have taken steps to save their lions. They set aside special land areas for them. These are known as game reserves. It is against the law to harm a lion there. Guests can only "shoot" lions with their cameras.

Tigers are in greater danger than lions. They have been very heavily hunted over the years. Even today, some of their body

There are many reserves in Africa where lions cannot be hunted.

parts are used in certain Chinese medicines. In recent years, steps have been taken to protect tigers, as well. Yet, they remain in serious danger of dying out.

Some tigers and lions have killed humans. But the numbers are clear—humans have killed far more lions and tigers. We remain the greatest threat to these animals.

Humans are the biggest threat to lions and tigers.

Fast Facts About
FIERCE CATS

❖ Tigers have caused more human deaths than any other big cat.

❖ Fewer than 2,000 tigers now remain in the wild.

❖ Since the start of the twentieth century, the tiger's territory has been reduced by 95 percent.

❖ There are far more Siberian tigers in zoos than in the wild.

❖ In some zoos, lions have been mated with tigers. Their young are called tigons.

❖ Lions are the most powerful members of the cat family.

❖ After a large meal, a lion may sleep for as long as a full day and night.

❖ In some ways, lions and tigers are like house cats. They spend much of the day sleeping. That is why daytime naps are called "cat naps!"

Glossary

coax	To urge gently.
corpse	A dead body.
game reserve	A specific area of land in which wildlife is protected.
livestock	Animals raised by farmers.
lure	To lead an animal into a trap.
predator	An animal that kills and eats other animals for food.
prey	Animals that are eaten by other animals as food.
pride	A group of lions that live together.
safari	A trip taken to hunt large wild animals.
scavengers	Animals that feed on dead animals.
scent	An odor left by an animal.
seize	To grab or take hold of.
shrine	A holy or honored place.
stalk	To hunt or track in a quiet or secret manner.
roam	To wander about.

Further Reading

Books

Darling, Kathy. *Lions*. Minneapolis, Minn.: Carolrhoda Books, 2000.

Fitzgerald, Patrick J. *Lion Attacks*. Danbury, Conn.: Children's Press, 2000.

Montgomery, Sy. *The Man-Eating Tigers of Sundarbans*. Boston: Houghton Mifflin, 2001.

Murdico, Suzanne J. *Tiger Attacks*. Danbury, Conn.: Children's Press, 2000.

Winters, Kay. *Tiger Trail*. Simon & Schuster, 2000.

Internet Addresses

Born Free Foundation's Big Cat Campaign
Learn interesting big cat facts.
<http://www.bornfree.org.uk/big.cat/index.html>

Big Cats Online
Offers a general introduction to the various species of cats living in the wild today.
<http://dialspace.dial.pipex.com/agarman/bco/ver4.htm>

Index

A

Africa, 24–29, 38, 43
attack, 9–12, 13, 14–15, 20, 21, 22–23, 24–28, 30, 31, 32–37, 44, 45

B

Bronx Zoo, 12–15
burial practice, 37

C

cat, 7, 8, 16, 18, 20, 23, 36, 37, 38, 41, 45
cattle, 41
Champawat, 33–35
Corbett, Jim, 35

D

Darkness, 25–29
deer, 22–24, 41

F

The Field Museum of Natural History, 27
fish, 31, 41

G

game reserve, 43
Ghost, 25–29
Gold, Jan, 7–12

I

India, 30–33, 34–35, 38

K

Kenya, 24–29

L

lion
    African, 13–15, 24–29, 38, 43
    color, 18, 20
    cub, 42–43
    diet, 19, 20–21, 24, 28, 29, 36, 37, 40–41, 42–43, 45
    habitat, 38, 39–40
    mating, 41–42, 45
    protection of, 43
    reserve, 30–33
    senses, 19
    size, 13, 18, 21, 42
    strength, 18, 21, 36, 45
    teeth, 19–20, 29, 36
lioness, 18, 40–41

M

man-eater, 33–35

N

Nepal, 33–34

P

parrot, 7
Patterson, John Henry, 26–27
prey, 9, 19, 20–21, 23–24, 29, 34, 36, 37, 41, 43

S

Southeast Asia, 31, 37
Sundarbans Tiger Reserve, 30–33

T

Tiaga, 8, 9–10, 11
tiger
    coat, 16–17, 20
    diet, 9, 19, 20–21, 23–24, 36, 37, 40–41, 42–43
    habitat, 17, 38–39, 45
    mating, 41–42, 45
    number of, 43
    protection of, 43–44
    senses, 19
    Siberian, 8–11, 45
    size, 8–11, 16, 18, 21, 42
    strength, 21, 36
tigon, 45
tigress, 16, 33–35, 39
Tsavo River, 25
Tundra, 8, 11

V

Vietnam War, 37

W

warthog, 41

Z

Zoo Boise, 7–11